Illness & Injury

Sylvia Goulding

CHERRYTREE
BOOKS

Published in 2006 by The Evans Publishing Group
2A Portman Mansions
Chiltern Steet
London W1U 6NR

© 2005 The Brown Reference Group plc.

Printed in China

British Library Cataloguing in Publication Data

Goulding, Sylvia
  Illness & injury. - (Healthy kids)
  1.Diseases - Juvenile literature 2.Wounds and injuries - Juvenile literature
  I.Title
  616

ISBN-10 paperback:	184234319X
ISBN-13 paperback:	9781842343197
ISBN-10 hardback:	1842344137
ISBN-13 hardback:	9781842344132

PHOTOGRAPHIC CREDITS
Cover: **The Brown Reference Group plc:** Edward Allwright
Title page: **The Brown Reference Group plc**: Edward Allwright
BananaStock: 23, 28, 29; **The Brown Reference Group plc**: Edward Allwright 3, 5, 6, 7, 8, 10, 12, 13, 18, 20, 22; **Corbis**: 5, 24, 26; **Hemera Photo Objects**: 11, 15, 17, 21; **Family Healthcare**: 4, 13, 25; **Simon Farnhell**: 4, 5, 7, 9, 15, 17, 19, 27; **Photos.com**: 19, 25.

FOR THE EVANS PUBLISHING GROUP

Editor: *Louise John*
Production: *Jenny Mulvanny*
Design: *D. R. ink*
Consultant: *Dr. Julia Dalton BM DCH*

FOR THE BROWN REFERENCE GROUP PLC

Art Editor: **Norma Martin**
Managing Editor: **Bridget Giles**

With thanks to models **Natalie Allwright, India Celeste Aloysius, Molly Camara, Zac Evans, Isabella Farnhell, Connor Thorpe, Joshua and Callum Tolley, Sam Thomson, and Isabella Trevisiol**

Important note: *Healthy Kids encourages readers to actively pursue good health for life. All information in* **Healthy Kids** *is for educational purposes only. For specific and personal medical advice, diagnoses, treatment and exercise and diet advice, consult your doctor.*

Some words are shown in bold, **like this**. You can find out what they mean by looking in the glossary on page 30.

Contents

Infectious diseases:
  Colds, flu and fever 4
Infectious diseases: Stomach upset 6
Breathing problems: Coughing 8
What are allergies? 10
Aches and pains 12
What is cancer? 14
Inherited diseases 16
First aid: Cuts, scrapes and burns 18
First aid: Broken bones 20
Pay attention... 22
At the doctor's 24
Staying in hospital 26
When you are getting better 28
Glossary 30
To find out more 30
Index 32

Infectious diseases:
Colds, flu and fever

Colds and flu are common **infectious** diseases. Both are caused by **viruses**. You breathe in viruses from the air in tiny droplets when someone near you sneezes or coughs. A cold or flu normally lasts about a week. There's no cure. **Antibiotics** cannot kill viruses. Cough medicine, throat lozenges and painkillers can make you feel better, but only take these when they are given to you by an adult.

◄ *Your normal body temperature is 37°C. You have a fever when your temperature is higher than that.*

rest

1

Or try this...

To help you breathe better...
● Put a few drops of peppermint oil in an **inhaler** like the one on the left. Breathe in deeply. Or add some drops to a bowl of warm water. Breathe in the steam from the bowl.
● Drip eucalyptus oil onto your pillow before you go to bed.

eat lots of fruit and vegetables.

Cold or flu?

When you have a cold...
A cold makes you feel unwell. You have a stuffy, runny nose. Your nose can also get sore. You may cough. And you may have a slight fever.

When you have flu...
Flu often feels much worse than a cold. You have an even higher temperature. It makes you feel shivery and tired. Your body feels achy.

Fevers...
See a doctor if your temperature is higher than 40°C or if your fever lasts for more than two days.

Strengthen your body's defences. Eat plenty of fresh fruit and vegetables to stay healthy.

▶ *A-choo! A cold makes you sneeze until your nose is red.*

drink lots of liquid

To soothe a sore throat...
● Drink plenty of liquid. Mix warm water with lemon juice and 1 tablespoon of honey.
● Gargle with 1 teaspoon of salt in warm water.

Infectious diseases:
Stomach upset

a stomach upset can make you feel very unwell. You lose your appetite. You feel sick. You might need to **vomit** or suffer from **diarrhoea**. If you feel like this, rest. When you vomit or get diarrhoea, your body loses a lot of water. Drink lots of water to replace the water you have lost and you'll soon feel much better. But take it easy at first.

◄ *Stomach cramps can come on suddenly. Most are mild, but some can be painful. If you are in great pain, see a doctor.*

rest in bed 1

Or try this...

When you feel really ill...
- Eat dry toast or soup for a day.
- Rest. If possible, lie in bed and sleep.
- Drink lots of water.

- Mix 4 cups of water, 1 teaspoon of salt and 8 teaspoons of sugar. Drink small amounts of this throughout the day.
- Try some weak camomile tea.

wash your hands before eating 3

What causes upsets?

▼ *When you feel sick, try eating dry toast or gingerbread biscuits. Ginger settles your stomach.*

Germs that make you sick...

Germs live in dirty places. They can get passed on from one person to another. Always wash your hands after you've been to the toilet, after you've stroked an animal and before you touch food.

Food that makes you sick...

Eating too much food can make you feel sick. You might feel unwell if you have eaten too many sweets or too much spicy food. Also, watch out for food that is past its sell-by-date.

▶ *Before you eat, wash your hands with soap and warm water.*

drink plenty of liquid

When you feel a little better...

● Follow the BRAT diet: **B**ananas, **R**ice, **A**pples and dry slices of **T**oast.
● Gradually return to eating normal food.

Breathing problems:
Coughing

Coughs sometimes start with a cold or flu. They can be painful and give you a sore throat. Even when the cold is gone, the cough may still be there. Coughing helps you clear your airways. It helps you cough up blockages, like **mucous** or dust. Often coughs are worse just after you've gone to bed and just after you've woken up.

◀ *Cover your mouth when you cough. This stops others getting ill.*

Or try this...

Ways to ease a cough...
- There are two types of cough syrup. **Suppressants** stop a dry cough. **Expectorants** loosen mucus so you can cough it up. Ask your doctor which is best for you to take.
- Suck a lozenge if your throat is sore.
- Drink lots of warm honey and water.

◀ *Inhalers help you breathe if you suffer from asthma.*

If you're unfit or overweight you may have breathing problems. Get active now to help you breathe better.

Out of breath...

You may be short of breath if...

...you have **asthma**. It narrows your airways. An inhaler widens them to help you breathe again.

You may have a cough if...

...you have a cold or another illness, for example **bronchitis** or **laryngitis**. Your doctor may give you antibiotics. If you have a fever, rest in bed.

You also cough if...

...you've breathed in dust, fumes or smoke.

▶ *If you have asthma, carry your inhaler with you.*

Breathe better...

● Sit up straight. Place one hand on your chest, the other on your stomach. Make sure your stomach goes out when you breathe in, but your chest stays still.

Safety first!

Visit your doctor if your cough...
● ...lasts for more than a week.
● ...is severe or gives you chest pains.
● ...makes you cough up blood.

What are...
Allergies?

an **allergy** fools your body into thinking that something that is usually harmless, like dust or pollen, is harmful. There are many types of allergies and it is possible to be allergic to things you touch, breathe in or eat. Some people are allergic to insect stings or medicine. An allergy can make you sneeze, give you a skin rash or even breathing problems. Allergies make some people very ill.

◄ *Some children are allergic to nickel, a metal. Nickel jewellery gives them a rash.*

Or try this...

If you know what you're allergic to...
● ...avoid that particular food or thing. Don't eat foods that make you allergic. Don't run in grass if you have hay fever.

To find out what you're allergic to...
● Write down what you touched or ate before you got ill.
● Ask your doctor for an allergy test.

Common allergies

One in every two hundred people in the UK are allergic to nuts.

23 million people in the UK suffer from allergies.

Touch allergies

Include some metals, pets, feathers, fur or washing powders. Can cause: a skin rash.

Food and drink allergies

Include wheat, eggs, nuts or milky foods. Can cause: rash, vomiting, stomach cramps, swollen lips, diarrhoea.

'Breathing' allergies

Include **pollution**, dust, **pollen** from trees, flowers or grass. Pollen allergy is called hay fever. Can cause: runny nose, sneezing, red and itchy eyes, asthma attacks.

▶ Some people are allergic to cats.

◀ Pollen often looks like a fine yellow dust. It is made by flowers.

Safety first!

See a doctor if, after eating...
- ...your mouth or body is itchy or swollen.
- ...you feel sick or have stomach pains.
- ...you're sneezy and have a runny nose.
- ...you get sudden diarrhoea.
- ...your muscles feel weak.

Call an ambulance if, after eating...
- ...someone falls over or stops breathing.

Aches and pains

pains are warning signals. They tell your brain that something is not right. Some pains are short and sharp; for example, if you cut or burn yourself. They go away when the wound heals. Other pains come from the inside of your body. Sometimes it's hard to tell exactly where you feel the pain. The pain could be sharp or dull. It may be there all the time. Or it may come in short bursts. It tells you something is wrong.

◀ *A headache might get better if you press a cold wet cloth against your head.*

Safety first!

See your doctor if you...
- ...have pain for more than a day.
- ...have a very high fever.
- ...bleed from a part of your body.

- ...have swollen **joints** or muscles.
- ...get more tired than normal.
- ...lose a lot of weight quickly.
- ...feel pain after taking medicine.

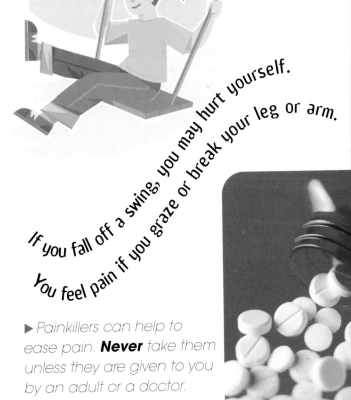

Avoiding pain...

Avoiding headache
Learn to relax. Sit better. Get exercise and fresh air. Sleep well. Drink lots of water. Get your eyesight checked.

Avoiding stomachache
Have a good breakfast. Eat healthy food, in small portions. Avoid too much spicy or sweet food.

Avoiding earache
Cover your ears if it's cold. Wear earplugs when you go swimming. Blow your nose or yawn on a plane. Don't ever put anything inside your ear.

If you fall off a swing, you may hurt yourself.
You feel pain if you graze or break your leg or arm.

▶ Painkillers can help to ease pain. **Never** take them unless they are given to you by an adult or a doctor.

Or try this...

Keep a pain diary...
- When and where do you feel pain?
- What does it feel like? Describe it.
- How strong is it? Give marks out of ten.

▶ A hot water bottle wrapped in a towel may ease earache.

What is cancer?

Cancer is a very serious disease. Different **cancers** attack different parts of the body, such as the lungs or the skin. Your body is made of millions of tiny building blocks called **cells**. Cancer makes cells copy themselves uncontrollably and these copies form **tumours**. Two cancers mainly affect children – **leukaemia**, which is a cancer of the blood, and brain tumours, which are lumps that grow inside the head.

◄ *A cancer patient sleeps in hospital.*

Safety first!

See your doctor if...

- ...you lose a lot of weight quickly.
- ...you have a mole that grows larger or changes colour or shape.
- ...there's blood in your urine or stool.
- ...you have a pain that won't go.
- ...you have a very bad headache.

Cancer treatments

Operations

In many cases, a **surgeon** can cut out a tumour.

Drug treatment

In **chemotherapy**, powerful drugs are given through a tube straight into the blood. It may take many weeks to work and can be very exhausting.

Ray treatment

Powerful rays are aimed at the body part that has cancer. This therapy is called **radiotherapy**. The rays kill cancerous cells.

▲ *If you have to stay in hospital for treatment, take some books along so you don't get bored.*

In hospital, you could try listening to some music through your headphones. It can be very relaxing.

What to do...

If you know someone with cancer...
- Don't shy away. Cancer is not catching.
- Visit them often and comfort them.
- Help them catch up with schoolwork.

▶ *Special nurses care for cancer patients.*

▼ Learn all about your
illness. It helps you to cope.

Inherited diseases

not all diseases are infectious. Some illnesses are passed down within a family. These are known as inherited diseases. This means that a child is born with a disease and someone else in their family, for example a parent or grandparent, probably has the same disease, too. **Cystic fibrosis** and **sickle-cell anaemia** are two well-known inherited illnesses.

Or try this...

Treating sickle-cell anaemia...
- A drug called **penicillin** and vitamin pills can prevent infections.
- Some children are given extra blood.

Treating cystic fibrosis...
- Special exercises help loosen and cough up the mucus in the lungs.
- Antibiotic drugs help with breathing.

◀ *A teddy bear can't make you better but it can help you feel less lonely.*

Ithy food, exercise and rest help to prevent children with inherited diseases from catching other infections.

Inherited diseases

You can learn to live happily with an inherited disease. But try not to catch an infection.

Cystic fibrosis

The body makes an extra sticky mucus. This clogs up the patient's lungs. Breathing gets difficult. The body finds it hard to break food down. The patient coughs a lot.

Sickle-cell anaemia

Blood cells are the wrong shape and get stuck in narrow blood vessels. Patients tire easily. They may feel pain in the bones, stomach or chest. This disease mainly affects people of African origin.

Ways to help yourself...
● Learn to watch your body for warning signals – fevers, pains and aches.
● Don't get too cold, hot or tired.

▶ *You are not alone. There's someone to comfort you most times.*

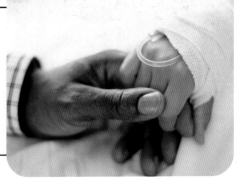

First aid:
Cuts, scrapes and burns

It's easy to get hurt when you're playing at home or outside. If you fall, you could scrape your knees. When you help in the kitchen, you could cut your finger on a knife. If you touch something hot, you could burn your hand. Many of these skin wounds are small. They can be treated at home. They heal quickly. But you need help with serious wounds.

▼ *A scrape may be dirty. Clean it well with cold water. Then stick on a plaster to keep dirt out.*

FIRST AID

Safety first!

Get help quickly if...
- ...the bleeding does not stop.
- ...a burn is larger than your hand.
- ...a fresh burn looks white or black.
- ...you're bitten by an insect
- ...you're bitten by a stray animal, such as a dog.
- ...your wound does not heal.

Treating a wound

Cuts

Rinse a small cut under water. Dab it dry with a clean cloth. Stick on a plaster. If the cut is deep, lie down. Hold that part of your body up and press on it to slow the bleeding. Ask for help.

Scrapes

Scrapes are painful but heal quickly. Make sure you wash out any dirt.

Burns and scalds

If you have a small burn, hold the burned area under cold, running water. Get help for serious burns.

Bite wounds

Get help. These wounds need to be treated by a first aider.

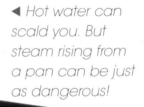

◀ *Hot water can scald you. But steam rising from a pan can be just as dangerous!*

◀ *Don't get friendly with pets you don't know. Some may bite.*

Just amazing!

Animal bites

About 200,000 dog bites occur each year in the UK. Most of these are from pets or animals that people know well!

Broken bones

falling is the main reason children break their bones. Hands, arms, feet, legs and the **collar bones** break most easily. You can't always tell from the outside if a bone is broken. It hurts a lot, especially when you touch it and it could be swollen. Sometimes the end of a broken bone sticks out. If you fall and it's very painful, get help. Ask to be taken to the hospital straight away. An **X-ray** of the bone shows whether it is broken or not (see p21).

◀ *A sling protects a broken arm on the way to the hospital or when it is nearly healed. It keeps your arm still while the bone is repairing itself. And it warns others to be careful around you.*

Safety first!

If you think you've broken a bone...
- ...move as little as possible.
- ...don't move at all if your back hurts.
- ...don't force the bone back into place.

- ...don't eat or drink anything in case you need an operation.
- ...ask others to call an ambulance and get you to a hospital quickly.

How they heal...

Straightening the bones

The doctor may put a **plaster cast** around your arm or leg. This keeps the broken bone straight and still. If the bone is broken into many pieces, you may need an operation.

Instant self-repair

Your body starts to repair a bone as soon as it breaks. The gap between the broken bits closes up.

On the mend

Normally it only takes a few weeks for your bones to heal. Take it easy when the plaster comes off – the new bone and your muscles are still weak.

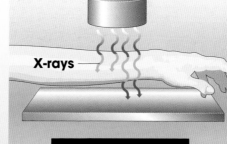

X-rays

bone — break

◀ *X-rays pass through skin but not bone. This creates a black and white image – an X-ray – of bones. This person's arm is broken.*

▶ *Plaster casts can be fun – you may even be able to choose a colour. Or you could get all your friends to sign the cast.*

Safety first!

Protect your bones...
● Wear helmets and knee pads on your bike, skateboard or skates.
● Always wear a seatbelt in the car.

Just amazing!

● Grown-ups have at least 210 bones in their body. Some have more bones than others in their skull, ribcage or back.

Pay attention...

Some children have problems concentrating at school. They can't sit still or listen for a long time. They fidget. They forget things. It's not because they're lazy or stupid – they might have **Attention Deficit Hyperactivity Disorder**, known as **ADHD** for short. A doctor can check this and medicine can often be given to help.

▶ *If you get very angry, don't have a tantrum. Count slowly to ten instead.*

Or try this...

Sleep better...
- Have quiet time before bed.
- Keep the lights low. Turn the TV off.
- Sleep in a quiet, dark room.

Learn to relax...
- Listen to some quiet, gentle music.
- Draw or paint a picture.
- Have a hot bath before going to bed.

Ways to help yourself

Some children with ADHD use medicines to help them. But there are other ways to help yourself get better.

Learn to care for a pet

Ask your parents if you can have a pet. Learn to look after it. It needs food and water. Its cage needs cleaning. Some pets need to be walked.

Get a hamster or rabbit. Learn to care for your pet.

▶ *Tidy away your books and see how easy it is to get a star!*

Keep a job diary

● Write down every part of every job you need to do. Write them in great detail like this: '1. Get up. 2. Take books. 3. Put books on the shelf'.

● Give yourself a star for everything you do. The more you write down, the more stars you can give yourself.

Or try this...

Learn to enjoy nature...

● A walk in the park can relax you.
● Spot new plants. What are they?
● Listen to sounds. What makes them?

At the doctor's

if you feel ill, you go to see your doctor. She will try to find out what is wrong with you. Once she knows, she can help you get better. The doctor will ask you lots of questions. Do you feel pain? Where and when is it painful? What does the pain feel like? When did your problem start? What did you eat before it started? The answers to these questions help the doctor to find out why you're ill.

◄*The doctor may check inside your mouth. She holds your tongue down. She shines in a light to see what's wrong.*

Or try this...

Before you go to see a doctor...
- ...think what feels wrong or painful.
- ...think when and why it started.
- ...think what you did just before.

More tests...
Sometimes, a doctor cannot find out by himself what is wrong. He may ask you to go to a hospital for more tests.

Tests doctors might do

Checking your body

A doctor may give you a check-up. What she does depends on what might be wrong with you. She could look into your mouth, eyes or ears. She might listen to your chest. She might feel your stomach. She could take your temperature.

Checking blood

Sometimes a doctor takes a small amount of blood from your finger or arm. This **sample** is then tested in a laboratory to check for problems.

Pictures of your inside

X-rays and **scans** are ways of taking photos of the inside of your body. They can show broken bones or other things that may be wrong.

A stethoscope is a doctor's special instrument for listening to your chest.

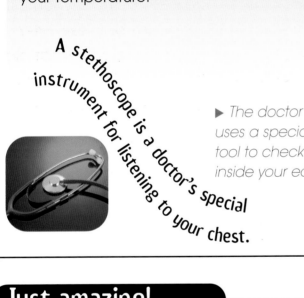

▶ *The doctor uses a special tool to check inside your ear.*

Just amazing!

Too late to help...

In ancient times, doctors had no X-rays. They often didn't know why a person was ill until after they had died.

Staying...
In hospital

there are lots of different types of hospitals for treating all sorts of different problems, illnesses and diseases. There are also special hospitals that are just for children. The doctors and nurses in these hospitals are specially trained to care for ill children. The three main reasons why children go into hospitals are for check-ups, for special treatment and care or for operations.

◀ *After a serious illness or an operation, you need to stay in hospital and take time to regain your strength.*

Or try this...

Things to do in the hospital...
- Be quiet. Don't disturb other people. They could be more ill than you.
- Try to sleep a lot. It will help you to get better, so you can go home.
- Eat and drink only what the doctor or nurse gives you. If you want to eat something else, ask them first.

◀ Pack your pyjamas, toothbrush, toothpaste, books, games and a favourite toy or teddy.

In a hospital

Inpatients

Some children stay in hospital for an operation or for treatment. They stay in bed most of the time – usually in a room with other children. They can have visitors most of the time.

▶ Staying in a hospital may be scary. But it's fun, too. There are lots of people to meet. And the doctors and nurses are always very friendly.

Preventing infection

Children with an infectious disease may have to stay in a room on their own. This is so other children don't get ill too.

Outpatients

Some children go to a day clinic. They can have check-ups or treatment. Afterwards, they can go straight home.

What is it?

A blood transfusion is...

...when another person's blood is dripped through a tube into your arm. You may need to have a transfusion if you lose a lot of blood in an operation, for example. Your body makes new blood on its own, but a transfusion can help until your body is well enough to do this.

When you are...
Getting better

When you've been ill, it takes a while to get your strength back. You can't go back to school or being active straight away. After a hospital stay, your doctor may tell you to rest at home for a while. Follow all the instructions she gives you. Finish taking the medicines you've been given. Eat only what you've been told to eat. Start sports again slowly, a little at a time.

◀ *Lie down and relax. Listen to your favourite music or read. Don't jump around yet if you're still weak.*

Test -?-?-?-?-?

1 When you feel better, you should...
A ...stop taking medicine right away.
B ...finish taking a course of medicine
C ...pass medicine to someone else.

2 After being ill in bed for a while...
A ...get fit slowly, a little each day.
B ...exercise as hard as you can.
C ...keep lying in bed all day.

Take it easy. Practise some slow moves like Tai Chi. It makes both your muscles and your mind strong.

▼ *Before you plan your next match, ask your doctor if it's okay for you to run around.*

Helping you...

Special exercises

To get better, some children need **therapy**. There are many types. **Physiotherapy**, for example, exercises stiff muscles after a broken bone has healed. Speech therapy helps you to speak better. Some other therapies help you to relax and make you feel good in your mind.

Learning new things

After an accident or illness, the medical staff can help you learn new ways of doing things. They might show you how to walk on crutches, for example. Or they may tell you which foods to avoid if you have an allergy.

3 To stay healthy, you should...

A ...eat lots of biscuits and sweets.
B ...drink buckets of fizzy drinks.
C ...eat fresh fruit and vegetables.

4 Before you go back to school...

A ...catch up on schoolwork you missed.
B ...read, draw, listen to music.
C ...get well and healthy.

Answers: 1B; 2A; 3C; 4A, B, and C

Glossary
What does it mean ?

allergy: *When your body reacts to something harmless (like milk or dust). An allergy causes rashes or sickness.*

antibiotics: *Medicines that kill harmful germs in your body.*

asthma: *A chest disease in which breathing can be difficult.*

Attention Deficit Hyperactivity Disorder (ADHD): *An illness that makes it very hard for the sufferer to concentrate.*

bronchitis: *An infection of the air passages between windpipe and lungs. It makes breathing hard. You cough a lot.*

cancer: *One of several serious diseases. Cells (tiny units that make up your body) copy themselves without control. This damages the body and forms tumours.*

cells: *The smallest building blocks in our body. Your body contains billions of cells.*

chemotherapy: *Treating cancer with drugs.*

collar bone: *A bone between the neck and the shoulders.*

cystic fibrosis: *A disease passed from parents to children. Sufferers find it hard to breathe. They cough a lot.*

diarrhoea: *A condition in which your stool is runny and you often need to go to the toilet.*

expectorant: *A type of cough medicine.*

infectious: *Something, such as certain illnesses, that is passed from person to person.*

inhaler: *A machine for breathing in medicine.*

joints: *The places where two bones meet.*

laryngitis: *An infection of the throat.*

leukaemia: *A cancer that affects the blood.*

mucous: *A sticky, wet liquid.*

penicillin: *A type of antibiotic. Some people are dangerously allergic to penicillin, though.*

physiotherapy: *A treatment for stiff muscles and pain. It includes rubbing and exercise.*

To find out more...

...read these books

- Powell, Jillian. *Like Me, Like You...Becky has Diabetes.* Evans Publishing Group, 2003.
- Parker, Steve. *Need to Know: Allergies.* Heinemann Library, 2004.
- Gale Buhler, Karen. *The Kids' Guide to First Aid: All About Bruises, Burns, Stings, Sprains and Other Ouches.* Williamson Publishing, 2002.
- *Look After Yourself* KS2 CD Rom. Evans 2006.

plaster cast: *A hard case that holds an arm, leg or other body part still. A plaster cast helps broken bones heal properly.*

pollen: *Tiny specks of dust made by flowers. Plants need pollen to make new plants.*

pollution: *Dirt in the air, water or earth. A lot of pollution is caused by people, cars, businesses and towns and cities.*

radiotherapy: *A treatment for cancer. Rays that kill cancer cells are aimed at the body.*

sample: *A small amount of blood, urine or stool. It can be checked for signs of illness.*

scans: *Computer pictures of the inside of the body.*

sickle-cell anaemia: *An inherited disease of the blood.*

suppressant: *A type of cough medicine.*

surgeon: *A doctor who does operations.*

therapy: *A treatment to help a sick or injured person get better.*

tumour: *A lump of cancerous cells.*

viruses: *Tiny particles that make you ill.*

vomit: *To be sick or throw up.*

X-ray: *A type of photograph that shows hidden things such as bones in the body.*

To find out more...

...check out these websites

- www.childrenfirst.nhs.uk/
- www.healthykids.org.uk/
- www.evelinakids.nhs.uk
- www.clic.org.uk/
- www.childrenfirst.nhs.uk/kids/
  health/illnesses/allergies/
  general.html

- Lennard-Brown, Sarah. *Health Issues: Asthma*. Hodder Wayland, 2005.
- *Shining On: A Collection of Stories in Aid of the Teen Cancer Trust*. Picadilly Press, 2006.
- Ganeri, Anita. *How My Body Works*. Evans, 2006.

Index

Which page is it on?

A
ache 12
ADHD 22, 23
allergic to food 11
allergic to touching 11
allergies 10, 11
allergy test 10
antibiotics 4, 9, 16
appetite 6
asthma 9, 10
attention 22

B
bite wound 18, 19
bleeding 18
blood transfusion 27
BRAT diet 7
breathing 8, 9, 10
breathless 4, 9
broken bones 20, 21, 25
bronchitis 9
burn 12, 18, 19

C
cancer 14, 15
cells 14
check-up 25
chemotherapy 15
colds 4, 5
collar bone 20
cough syrup 4, 8
coughing 8, 9
cut 12, 18, 19
cystic fibrosis 16, 17

D
defences 5
diarrhoea 6, 11
doctor 9, 11, 12, 14, 24, 25
drink 5, 6
dust 8, 9, 11

E
earache 13
earplugs 13
expectorant 8

F
falls 13, 18
fevers 4, 5, 9
flu 4, 5
food 7, 11

G
germs 7
getting better 28, 29

H
hay fever 10, 11
headache 12, 13
hospital 14, 15, 26, 27
hot water 19

IJ
inhalers 4, 9
inpatients 27
job diary 23

L
laryngitis 9
learning 16, 29
leukaemia 14
lozenge 4, 8

MN
mucous 8
nature 23

OP
operation 15, 26, 27
outpatients 27
pain 12, 13
pain diary 13
pets 11, 19, 23
physiotherapy 29
plaster cast 21
pollen 11
pollution 11
protecting bones 21

R
radiotherapy 15
rash 10, 11
relaxing 22, 28

S
sample 25
scalds 19
scans 25
scrapes 18, 19
sick 4, 5, 6, 7
sickle-cell anaemia 16, 17
skin wounds 18
sleep 22
sneeze 4, 5, 10, 11
sore throat 5, 8
special exercises 29
staying in hospital 26, 27
steam 4, 19
stethoscope 25
stomachache 6, 7, 13
suppressant 8
surgeon 15
surgery 26
swimming 13

T
temperature 4, 5
tests 25
therapy 29
tumours 14, 15

VW
viruses 4
vomit 6
washing hands 7
wounds 18, 19

X
X-ray 20, 21, 25